TENNESSEE

PHOTOGRAPHY BY EDWARD SCHELL

TEXT BY WILMA DYKEMAN

Wilma Dykeman

International Standard Book Number 0-9613859-3-6

Copyright © 1979 by Graphic Arts Publishing Co.

Publisher: 1986 edition • Wakestone Books
405 Clifton Heights, Newport, Tennessee 37821

This book authorized and published under special arrangement with Graphic Arts Center Publishing Company in Portland, Oregon.

Printed in the United States of America

Right: The beautiful American lotus adapts to shallow lakes and quiet backwaters. It is now established on Bays Mountain, near Kingsport.

Misty mornings are a special delight along the rural highways and byways. Rise early and go leisurely, pausing frequently to savor the scene. Left: Layered and spread by the winds, colored and flamed by the sun, the evening clouds present an ever-changing world. Pages 8 and 9 following: Wind-stripped branches of yellow birches soar skyward on sunny autumn day.

Sunset at Neville Bay, Land-Between the Lakes, comparable to famed alpenglow of snow-capped mountains. Right: Fall foliage adds brilliance to young birch tree as it emerges from sheer rock wall, near Burbank. Pages 12 and 13 following: Silhouetted by light from the setting sun, ridgetop trees etch their shapes on the dimming sky, near Hampton.

Blooming of mountain rosebay or Catawba rhododendron on Roan Mountain in late June, heralds the annual Rhododendron Festival. Left: Buzzard's Roost at Fall Creek Falls State Park, is typical of bluffs above stream-carved valleys of the Cumberland Plateau.

Small waterfall, wind-ripples
and foaming raceways make
mountain streams a peaceful
retreat to escape the abrasions
of urban life. Right: Spring
comes to the Smokies along
Roaring Fork Nature Trail,
near Gatlinburg.

A lacelike fencerow in a hill country pasture, stands forth from the copper-toned sky of a late winter's eve, north of Johnson City. Left: Fir trees are determined to survive as they face the forces of nature on Roan Mountain.

An almost unbelievable texture, akin to finely crafted tapestry, clothes beech-maple climax forest. Right: Sundered by lightning, twisted and gnarled by gale-force winds, an ancient beech depicts life in the face of adversity atop a knob, in Southern Appalachia.

Leaves of white violets and
grasses array themselves on the
base of a southern balsam
stump, in Cherokee National
Forest. Left: Morrell Cave near
Bluff City is typical of many
limestone caverns in the state.
Spelunking or cave exploring
is a popular pastime. Pages 24
and 25 following: Broad
expanse of the Mississippi
River, our western boundary,
driving to the gulf draining
the continent's heartland.

Lights of Knoxville include the University of Tennessee from Cherokee Bluffs, above Fort Loudoun Lake, on the Holston River. Right: Yellow sneeze-weed gird a hawse-ring on the cobble-stoned riverboat wharf at Memphis. Pages 28 and 29 following: Twin trunks of a double sycamore soar skyward in a Washington county farm lot.

Great forests of white pine that awed early explorers are long-gone, but nature may once again restore our wilderness preserves. Right: The state has more than its share of wintering bald eagles. They are lured to lakes and streams of the Tennessee Valley, and particularly to Reelfoot Lake, when waters to the north are iced over.

Wind-sculptured snow along Little Pigeon River in the Great Smokies. Left: Snow dusts the trunks of young sycamores by the edges of the state's numerous rivers.

The Appalachian Trail exerts a powerful charm over outdoor enthusiasts. From an easy footpath to a rugged climb, it maximizes a confrontation with nature. Right: Leaves of Fraser's magnolia pass from green to brown-mottled yellow and finally to brown before they fall.

Morning sun and clouds in the Tennessee Valley. Left: 400 million years of geological history lie exposed on cliffs below scenic Fall Creek Falls. The falls prompted the development of a 16,000 acre state park by the same name.

Early summer dates arrival of rare sweetbay magnolia in wetlands near Ducktown and westwardly near Selmer. Right: Buck and doe at Bays Mountain near Kingsport. The deer herd at Cades Cove in the Smokies, excels in visible display of wild game. Pages 40 and 41 following: Hikers on Appalachian Trail cross Mt. Kephart headed for Charlie's Bunion. Early morning view from 6,593 foot, Mt. Le Conte in the Great Smokies.

Windblown sedges, grasses, rocky outcrops of granite and gneiss harmonize with balds of Appalachia. Right: Remnants of old settler's home on Ripshin Mountain remind one of the recent pioneers of the southern mountains. Pages 44 and 45 following: Sun-golden leaves and foliose lichens adhere to elderly sugar maple in mountain pasture.

Two oak leaves along a stream in the Appalachians. Right: Beech forests are among the greatest gifts of nature. They occur throughout the state and achieve maximum beauty during October.

The American bittern migrates through the state. When disturbed, it raises its bill to mimic the grasses of its marsh habitat and sways in harmony with the wind. Left: Fall foliage frames the waterfall at The Sinks of the Little River in the Great Smokies.

A relaxing trail to Abrams Falls parallels Abrams Creek, one of the Smokies' most beautiful streams. Right: A small stream of foaming white-water has eroded this autumn-burnished valley.

Old hawthorn tree near state line on 6,285 foot Roan Mountain overlooking 6,684 foot Mt. Mitchell in neighboring North Carolina. Left: Bessie Bend once harbored a Confederate battery preventing Union ships from passing downstream. Today it is a haven of serenity and peaceful beauty.

Cades Cove features the more recent pioneering activities, including Tipton-Oliver house built shortly after the Civil War. Right: Memorial to Andrew Jackson, the nation's hero of the war of 1812 and seventh president of the United States, on capitol grounds, Nashville. Pages 56 and 57 following: Morning sky, Great Smokies, from 6,642 foot Clingman's Dome, the highest point in the state.

Winter snows emphasize
leafless saplings along pastoral
fencerows, near Hampton.
Right: Rime ice occurs most
often in the higher mountains,
but can occur on rare occasions
throughout the state. Pages 60
and 61 following: Evening
light illuminates the water and
outlines cypress knees at
Reelfoot Lake.

Rare orchid of the broad-leaved forests is large yellow lady-slipper. Left: High sun over Chimneytops lights the translucent leaves and emphasizes textures of autumn forest in the Great Smoky Mountains.

Along the Mississippi, levees are stabilized by native grasses that reach perfection in late summer. Right: Ramsey cascades are reached after lengthy hike through a virgin wilderness of tulip, hemlock, and buckeye trees, in Great Smoky Mountain National Park.

William Christopher Handy, "father of the blues", and Beale Street are inseparable symbols of a uniquely American style of music. His first published composition was "Memphis Blues". Left: Lotus seed heads at Reelfoot Lake. The lake was created by the new Madrid Earthquake in 1811. The land sank and was filled by the waters of the Mississippi which flowed backwards during the quake.

Chucalissa Indian village, on a
bluff above the Mississippi, was
originally built about 1,000 A.D.
Chucalissa is a Choctaw word
meaning "abandoned houses".
Right: Spring beauty is found
from the Mississippi eastward
in April and May; acres of white
blossoms carpet the beech gaps
of the higher mountains.

Dome building adds a unique bit of Americana to the Chattanooga scene. Left: Burgess Falls on the Falling Water River near Cookeville plunges directly into Center Hill Lake. Pages 72 and 73 following: The Great Smokies in early morning from 6,642 foot Clingman's Dome.

Lichen-covered rocks on Lookout Mountain at Moccassin Bend in Tennessee River with Chattanooga beyond. Left: All Saints Chapel at University of the South features revered stained glass. Its academic program has produced many Rhodes scholars. Pages 76 and 77 following: Product of limestone soils is the red cedar. The aroma when burning, surpasses that of choice oriental incense.

Golden ragwort blankets mountain pasture in late April, signalling the annual Carter County Wildflower Tour. Right: Haircap mosses lay a rich green carpet throughout the forests. and nearby streams.

A song sparrow feeds its young in a red cedar tree. Left: Massive specimens of tulip tree on the Ramsey Cascades Trail in the Great Smokies. There are few places left, where uncut forests of our state tree still thrive.

Sunrise from Mt. Le Conte deep in the heart of the Great Smokies. Le Conte Lodge located nearby, provides accommodations and meals carried in on horseback, for those wishing this attention. Right: Mid-spring dictates arrival of blooming dogwood and redbud, when Johnson City's beauty trails and Knoxville's Dogwood Arts Festival, show the cities in their finest.

Old stump provides a habitat
for young firs, lichens, mosses,
fungi and insect larvae to satisfy
the birds, as it slowly decom-
poses. Right: The village of
Burbank typifies the peaceful
isolation of many small
mountain towns.

Flood-ravaged willow, canti-
levered from the Arkansas
shore, overlooks the Hernando
De Soto Bridge and Memphis
on the Mississippi River. Right:
Virginia creeper, one of the
loveliest of wild vines occurs
throughout the state. Pages 88
and 89 following: Frosted
forest on a high ridge along the
Appalachian Trail.

Rimed branches and twigs of
young yellow birches stand out
against an indigo sky in
Cherokee National Forest.
Right: Gnarled hawthorn tree,
shaped by the wind, atop a bald
in the eastern highlands.
Pages 92 and 93 following:
Summer mists, tinged by golden
glow of the rising sun, collect
in the Doe River valley to
depart by mid-morning.

Abandoned bridge along
the Doe River near Hampton
is reclaimed by the forest.
A century hence man will see
no evidence of this span. Left:
Bald cypress, a magnificent
tree of the Mississippi Valley
is often found in shallow lakes,
ponds and wetlands, viewed
here at Reelfoot Lake.

96

Fancher's Falls plunges from a small creek into pool that drains into Center Hill Lake, near Sparta. Left: Rock outcrop on one of the many mountain balds, displays labor of nature, as lichens, mosses and woody plants transform rock into forest-covered soil, on Roan Mountain, near the Appalachian Trail.

More than 35 species of
goldenrods color the mountains
and gild the fields in late
summer. Right: Fontaine House,
restored French-Victorian
mansion retaining flavor
of bygone era in Memphis.

Columbine emerges from rich rocky soils of the eastern mountains, but also occurs near Nashville. Left: Red leaves of blueberry bush in late autumn along the Elk River. Pages 104 and 105 following: Grassy Ridge Bald viewed from Appalachian Trail on Roan Mountain is outstanding example of natural balds of southern Appalachians.

A full spectrum of sun colors
emerges from mist at the base
of a small waterfall, near Erwin.
Left: The bronze of the beech
tree is both bold and subtle.
Basically a strong brown,
the foliage sets it apart from
all other trees in the forest.
Pages 108 and 109 following:
Like an island in a sea of clouds,
the Black Mountains emerge,
looking south from 6,285 foot
Roan Mountain.

Covenant College sits astride
Lookout Mountain in this early
morning view from Raccoon
Mountain. Right: Sunrise,
Kentucky Lake, on the
Tennessee River,
Land-Between-the-Lakes.

Summer storm showers down
on summit of Roan Mountain
viewed across the grassy sweeps
from Jane Bald. Left: Fall brings
delicate mini-scenes to the
many little streams that flow
east of the Tennessee River.

Brilliant flame azalea blooms
in mid-June on a mountain bald
along the Appalachian Trail
passing 6,285 foot Roan High
Knob. Right: Birdsfoot violets
sometimes occur with upper
two petals a deep pansy-purple.
The top flower is tri-colored
as upper petals are tipped with
an intermediate hue.

On a peaceful fall morning,
it is difficult to imagine the
bloodshed enacted on Lookout
Mountain during the Civil War.
Left: Richly colored lichens,
born to survive on rocky
outcrops in exposed locations.

TENNESSEE

"Now it's a fact, nature has been mighty open-handed with us." The Tennessee mountain man leans back in his chair against the porch railing and looks at his visitor with eyes as bright and brown as a chinquapin. "Nature provided us with water a-plenty to quench our thirst, land a-plenty to feed ourselves—at least in most places—and then she threw in some pretties to lighten our spirits."

His visitor looks at the nearby sparkling stream plunging down the narrow valley, at the green patches of corn and "garden-truck" tended between house and barn, and at the distant ranges of mountains piled up along the horizon like frozen blue waves, and understands. Food for body and spirit.

Which is the season and right direction to find Tennessee?

Is it in the freshness of spring when redbud and dogwood splash the greening landscape with generous blossom, when the chartreuse mantillas of weeping willows stir like delicate lace under sudden gusts of wind, pastures assume emerald mantles of grass and newly plowed fields yield the pungent aroma of moist, rich earth? Is it in the luxuriance of summer with heat simmering above long rows of soybeans and cotton, corn and tobacco, mourning doves calling during long afternoons and a mockingbird singing during the long, languid night? Is it the fullness of autumn with every woods, even to patches of second-growth shrubs, blazing in rich scarlets and golds; with bins and barns bursting with harvest, and hunters out for birds and deer and fierce wild boar? Is it the stillness of winter with every scar on the land revealed in clear and definite detail, with green-boughed balsam trees bearing heavy burdens of pristine snow and ancient oak trees standing stripped and sturdy under onslaughts of storm sweeping in from the west and north?

Is it along the interstate highways that stretch straight and efficient like unrolled bandages between hillside cuts, severed farms, meadows, forests, towns, or along the narrow roads that wind and loop between upland knobs and lowland fields, crossroads stores, state parks, and raw little golf courses springing up like mushrooms around towns' edges? Is it at the courthouses dominating the county seats with their central imposing presence of authority and memory—authority for today's semblance of law and justice and an orderly relationship between the individual and society, memory stored in hundreds of fading volumes of deeds and wills, records of marriage, birth, death, and ceaseless transfer of property? Is it at the churches dotting the countryside, prominent along downtown thoroughfares, signifying formal (and sometimes very informal) religious commitments and relationships, the call of a steeple bell reaching across Sunday morning stillness, the sound of a hymn sung at Wednesday night prayer meeting?

Is it the throb and excitement of Saturday afternoon reaching toward the country or bluegrass or disco or blues or jazz or Elvis sound of Saturday night ranging from the plush luxury of the Grand Old Opry auditorium to the dingy alley honky-tonks of hundreds of small towns and rural back roads? Is it the Monday morning pilgrimage to sprawling industries and small plants multiplying in the countryside or to the fields atop machinery where patient mules once plodded? Is it the ritual of Sunday fried chicken, hot biscuits and iced tea, family reunions in late summer and early autumn?

Is it on mountains scarred and scalped by gouging augers and shovels tearing out long seams of coal? Is it on mountains still forested where blue shadows lengthen during winter afternoons and create a landscape mysterious as the moon? Is it along thoroughfares degraded by litter and junkyards and uncontrolled billboards to runways of ugliness, or is it along the passages fringed with grass, with trees, with people's homes and places of work? Is it in one name or a hundred, names that stir memory, conscience, imagination: Sycamore Shoals, Cumberland Gap, Natchez Trace, the Hermitage, Shiloh, Missionary Ridge, Copperhill, Norris, Oak Ridge.

Tennessee, of course, is each of these places and seasons.

Situated at the exact center of the eastern United States, Tennessee's domain stretches from the Great Smokies to the great river. That is the first fact fundamental to understanding this paradoxical and fascinating state.

Its weather, its flora and fauna relate to both New England and the Deep South. So do its people. In vintage political oratory one of its 19th century governors asserted that in this state the north and the south were wedded. "Tennessee," Governor Bob Taylor thundered, "lies on the happiest lines of latitude and longitude which girdle the globe; she lies on the dividing line between the two great agricultural regions of the world. On the south are the tropical fruits and flowers and cotton-fields, where labor toils and sings and tosses the snowy bales by the million into the lap of commerce. On the north are the fruits and cereals of the north temperate zone, where industry smiles and pours its streams of amber and gold into the garners of nations. But Tennessee combines them both. The pecans of the South fall among the hickory-nuts of the North on her soil. The magnolia blooms in the same grove where the Northern apple ripens, and the Georgia plum woos the blushing peach of Delaware. Corn and cotton, blue-grass and wheat, all grow in adjoining fields, while the mockingbird and the snowbird sing and chatter together on bough and bush away down in Tennessee."

Remembering that these words were delivered in the bitter aftermath of Civil War, perhaps the purple prose had a serious healing purpose as well as a personal political utility.

From mountain pinnacles to the Mississippi plain, Tennessee's geography and geology, natural history and human events embrace a diversity that is rare and picturesque, nurturing necessary adaptations that may degenerate into dangerous antagonisms, begetting tensions that may be usefully creative or exasperatingly destructive. Ancient geological tensions and awesome upheavals of the earth's crust that brought Tennessee's mountains and twisting erratic river-courses into being find their human counterpart in the east-west, north-south tensions that brought war's upheavals and sometimes violent change to the very hearths of the state's citizens.

Contrasts abound. To the east, in the land-locked coves of the Great Smokies and the Unakas and the Cumberlands, the horizon is near and awesome, defined by rugged pinnacles that may reach a height of more than 6,000 feet. This is a green secret world lavish with moss and ferns, tangled rhododendron and laurel, stately stands of poplar and oak, hickory, ash, maple, walnut, locust, and dozens of other trees including the evergreens that crown ridge-tops and mantle selected valley slopes. Streams fed by nature's underground reservoirs and clear springs—"bold and pure," their owners boast—splash down steep slopes and over boulder-strewn beds, gather other rivulets unto themselves, growing toward the rivers.

Approximately 432 miles westward, on the plateau of the Mississippi, the horizon stretches level and far toward the setting sun. This is a quiet landscape of bluffs overlooking the fields whose fertility has been fed through many centuries by the big river's overflow, where marsh and swamps offer another, hidden aspect of the river country's character, and the shallow waters of Reelfoot Lake reflect the dead snags of gum and willow and black walnut trees, as well as the gnarled knees and mighty trunks of living cypresses that flourish here. Wild grape and other looping, twisting vines weave draperies through the swamp timber and many varieties of grasses provide food for the water fowl that frequent these sites. The lakes and marshes contain quiet water, somnolent as much of the land, but all dominated by the majestic surge and sweep of the river driving to the Gulf, draining the continent's heartland.

Between these borders, each majestic in its own way, lies the highland rim and central basin of Middle Tennessee, a terrain of rough hills, deep valleys, the Tennessee and Cumberland rivers, and some of the most productive soil in the state. These rolling midlands are predominantly livestock country and stretch south from adjoining Kentucky with which they share much the same landscape. Caves and underground passages carved by water working on soft limestone are a feature of this region. Limestone also contributes to the rich cover of famous bluegrass that is distinctive here. Although Kentucky is called the Bluegrass State, Tennessee has about as many acres of that valuable grass. During year-round grazing it nourishes strong bones inherent in the noted Tennessee Walking Horses.

Even before it achieved statehood in 1796, the country contained in Tennessee inspired many responses in many people.

To Indians of numerous northern and southern tribes it was the pleasant hunting ground, opulent with water and succulent cane, salt licks and forests and meadows that attracted herds of buffalo and elk and deer, wild fowl and animals and fish species in rich and harmonious variety.

To the first European, hard-bitten, gold-hungry Hernando de Soto and his arrogant, courageous soldiers in their heavy clanking armor, spurring their Spanish horses across the unknown interior land of the South, herding their live commissary of rooting, squealing hogs and their retinue of captured Indian slaves, the country that would someday be western Tennessee became their last hope for glittering treasure. It was hope that disappeared with their leader's death and committal to the depths of the Great River, as they called the Mississippi.

To early English governors who claimed as part of the Virginia colony all the land from the Atlantic "westward to the South Sea," this interior country beyond the looming barrier of the hazy blue mountains offered, in 1626, "great hope both for the riches of the mountains and probabilities of finding the passage to the South Sea."

To James Needham who, in the spring of 1673, "adventured where never any English man had dared to attempt before," the Tennessee country was a "region of mystery that lay behind the mountain chains and on the western waters," and he lost his life in his discovery of the Valley of Tennessee.

To the Jesuit Father, Jacques Marquette, and the furtrader, Louis Jolliet of Quebec, who launched the first French exploration of the Mississippi River in the same season chosen by Needham at the opposite end of the state-yet-to-be, the spring of 1673, the Tennessee country viewed from their birch canoes along its westernmost boundary offered a feeling of solitude and grandeur, "a joy I cannot express," Father Marquette wrote.

To the Utopian dreamer, Christian Priber, the Tennessee country of the Overhill Cherokee among whom he went to live in 1736 was a perfect refuge after flight from his native Germany and sojourns in England and South Carolina. A refuge where he could finally lay the foundation for his proposed Kingdom of Paradise in which each citizen "would find what he needed" and "each should contribute to the good of the society as he could."

To able and learned Virginian Dr. Thomas Walker, in 1750, the vast area stretching from the Appalachian range to the Mississippi Valley was public domain waiting for development by the Loyal Company of which he was a dedicated member and for which he would survey and encourage settlement on "the Western Waters."

To Scotch-Irish and English traders entering Indian villages and hunting grounds in the early and mid-1700's, this teeming wilderness kindled dreams of wealth beyond calculation.

To Jamie, a black slave, 18 years old, for whom history has recorded no last name, only an account of his skill and courage in keeping alive for three months the severely injured member of a scouting party, the Tennessee country was bear, deer, small game for meat and clothing (Jamie may be the first recorded pioneer on the Southern frontier to wear a coonskin cap); it was persimmons and chestnuts for food, vines and cane for baskets, herbs for medicine; to both men it was challenge of mutual survival in raw wilderness.

To Andre Michaux and his son, French botanists for their king, the Tennessee country of the 1790's was a treasury of plant life in a variety and abundance seldom encountered elsewhere in the world.

To the Duke of Orleans who eventually became Louis Philippe, King of France, the Tennessee he found on a tour of 1797 was "a most lonely and desolate land," where the forests were beautiful but monotonous, the luxuriance of the river meadows was charming but the cooking at the inns and homes was inferior to that of "the smallest village in France."

To Daniel Boone, William Bean, John Sevier, and hundreds of other Virginians and Carolinians—English, Scotch-Irish, German, French Huguenot, Welsh, occasionally Swiss or Polish or of other nationality—this "land of the Western Waters" was just that: land; land in all its contradictory connotations of home and speculation, roots and adventure, risk and security.

Pleasant hunting ground, mirage of El Dorado, region of mystery or grandeur, illusion of Utopia, speculator's paradise, challenge for survival, botanist's dream, royalty's despair, vision of home: each was born of the Tennessee landscape and became part of its people's experience.

Writing of the Cumberland River as it loops across north-central Tennessee, contemporary historian-novelist Hariette Simpson Arnow evokes the sense of home and the nature of learning that was shaped by land and water from her youth.

"My people loved the past more than their present lives, I think, but it cannot be said we lived in the past. Two things tied all time together; these had run through most of the old stories to shape the lives of men, and so did they shape our lives and the lives of the people about us. These were the land and the Cumberland."

Heroes and events were made personal and "pin-pointed by running water," she recalls, and spins off associations a child might remember from history related by remembering elders: "Andrew Jackson had had a store on Stone's River, not far from the Cumberland; the Long Hunters and Daniel Boone had spent much time down around Mill Springs; Davie Crockett lived a while down on Obey's River, not so far from Wolf River where the father of Mark Twain, Marshall Clemens, lived; he had used to visit relatives over in Kentucky, and had a store and a 'great boundary' of land. Later, there were other names: Sergeant Alvin C. York was also from the Wolf River Country and Cordell Hull had grown up by the Cumberland, and no different than a large number of other farm boys had ridden log rafts down to Nashville."

Lonely and abundant, inviting and indifferent, this seems always to have been a landscape that spawned legends—of a spirit world for the earliest inhabitants, of scoundrels and heroes for later settlers. Land and water were at the center of the red Tennessean's legends and beliefs. They incorporated a sense of wonder and humor, daily familiarity surrounded by unfathomable mystery. Underneath the ground lived water-sprites who could bring forth springs and streams. Fierce bird-like creatures called Raven Mockers were harbingers of death. The world of mountains where a person's life could be lost by a single misstep on a rocky ledge or in the brooding swamps where a lurking cottonmouth could bring down the stoutest warrior, the power of the thundering buffalo and the plenty of plump pigeons that darkened the day with their flights: these and all other of nature's bounties and terrors the red tribes held in respect.

In their belief, the earth was "a great island floating in a sea of water." At first, when the earth was soft and wet, a great buzzard flew over the Cherokee country, "he was very tired and his wings began to slap and strike the ground, and wherever they struck the earth there was a valley, and where they turned up again there was a mountain."

After the earth was molded to its present shape, forms of life began to assume their unique characters. For instance, it was told that the animals and plants, soon after they were first made, were instructed "to watch and keep awake for seven nights." Some did well enough at first but by the seventh night "only the owl, the panther, and one or two more were still awake. To these were given the power to see and go about in the dark, and to make prey of the birds and animals which must sleep at night. Of all the trees only the cedar, the pine, the spruce, the holly, and the laurel were awake to the end, and to them it was given to be always green and to be greatest for medicine, but to others it was said: 'Because you have not endured to the end you shall lose your hair every winter.' "

Most of the cultural life of the Indians of Tennessee, their interpretation of the world around them and their relationship to it and to each other, remained unknown to the majority of white strangers. Archaic Indians here used the woods and caves, stone, bone, shell, reeds, and hides of animals long before civilizations emerged in the Nile and Euphrates valleys. Here were large earthworks or mounds whose origin remained a mystery to Europeans, giving rise to many theories of "Mound Builders," a separate and distinct race of people, now discounted by archaeologists. Standing on one of these earthworks, or at the most impressive—the Old Stone Fort at the forks of the Duck River near Manchester—on a late autumn afternoon with fading sunlight slanting across the landscape, surrounded by silence except for the call of a crow or a bluejay in the distance, pondering our ignorance of the history, the purposes, the meaning of this earth piled up, arranged, designed so long ago, a person's imagination may be stirred to wonder about the past.

The natives who were in Tennessee when the first Europeans arrived were members of those Southeastern tribes who, according to anthropologist Charles Hudson, "possessed the richest culture of any of the native people north of Mexico." It represents an incredible loss that they have been "the victims of a virtual amnesia in our historical consciousness." During those early centuries of encounter, European intellectuals found it difficult to communicate with even a noble "savage," and the Indians in their turn found it impossible to overcome European weapons and microbes and social disruption of all that had seemed orderly and true. Within some 300 years after de Soto slashed and burned and looted his way to the Chickasaw Bluffs of the present Memphis, the Indians had been subjugated militarily, become dependent on European trade goods, and pushed aside in national conscience.

Also pushed aside and lost was a cultural heritage richer than we may comprehend, in which humans and all other forms of life were interrelated parts of a great whole. Plants and animals and humans served each other, and when one was used for the well-being or survival of the other amends to the spirit were required. Men and women might not understand every aspect of the world around them but they felt related to its totality. Fragmentation of white civilization, with its spirit of conquest over nature, was alien to the red natives.

Our more scientific accounts of the shaping of mountains and valleys, the appearance of plant and animal life, are less poetic than the Indian's but they may also kindle a sense of awe as our minds try to comprehend elemental forces of heat and cold, water and rock, locked in a relentless struggle over a sweep of time so vast it is submerged in a distant dawn.

The mountains of Tennessee are ancient. Some of them were old when the Rockies and the Sierra Nevada were born. Geologists reckon the age of the Ocoee series of rocks that prevails in the Great Smokies at more than 500 or 600 million years, so aged that they provide no plant or animal fossils. At the beginning of the Paleozoic era 300 million years ago marine life stirred in shallow inland seas and the first forests began to emerge. Deposits gradually initiated the long process of laying down beds of materials for limestone and coal, accumulations that would become, in later eras, major influences on human habitation of the region.

Throughout these immense expanses of time, mountains were created in volcanic eruptions from the earth's interior, pushed up in massive wrinklings of the earth's crust. As other stresses and strains developed, the land was folded and faulted, violent upheavals thrust older layers of rock on top of later deposits. The countenance of Tennessee as we see it today, much like that of an elderly man or woman, reflects the never-ending interplay of relentless duration and change.

In this drama of cataclysmic strains and overthrow, gradual accretion and sudden revolution, land and water engaged in their constant deep-seated hatred. Streams and rivers seeking passages through mountain walls gouged out corridors and valleys. Tiny drops of water in constant flow, freezing and thawing, wore rocks away, sculpted the landscape. Where deposits were of marble—future source of one of East Tennessee's major industries and many of the nation's handsome edifices—water chiseled slowly indeed. Where there was limestone (it is said that limestone is a poor fighter) water formed the caves and sinkholes and narrow gorges that especially characterize the mid-state terrain. Varying kinds of rocks and soils, and an abundant rainfall were not the only agents carving out Tennessee's geography. In recent times the oldest force of all asserted its power once more.

On December 16, 1811, and for many days thereafter, until March 15, 1812, the earth in the Chickasaw Indian country of northwestern Tennessee was shaken by a series of tremors that tumbled land, trees, streams, in a gigantic upheaval. Deafening noise and the strong stench of sulphur that accompanied the earthquake intensified the fears of people scattered through the area that the Day of Judgment was upon them. The sound of prayers and hymns mingled with the squeaking rumbles of wagon wheels as the faithful loaded up their worldly possessions and fled.

Their terror was well-founded, as was their thankfulness that the major portion of destruction had taken place in a wilderness expanse of luxuriant forest and small water-courses near the Kentucky line. The dense forests of oak, elm, walnut, poplar, and cypress that had discouraged early settlement in the region were uprooted by the thousands. Cottonwoods 18 to 20 inches thick snapped and whirled away. River banks crumbled as landslides devoured the bluffs. Where the earth sank, the Mississippi River reversed its course and surged north in tumultuous waves to completely engulf the newly created basin. The New Madrid earthquake, as it was named, had created shallow Reelfoot Lake: 18 miles long, two-and-a-half miles wide, covering 25,000 acres. Just as its birth had provided a modern glimpse of the ancient drama of geological forces in action, so its name preserved the imaginative interpretations of Indians in the region.

On the bluffs along the Mississippi in the Chickasaw Nation it was told there lived a chief whose son was club-footed. The peculiar rolling gait with which he walked brought him the name Kalopin or Reelfoot. It also alienated him from courtship and marriage in his own tribe. He traveled to the country of the neighboring Choctaws and there, smoking the peace pipe with chief Copish, he fell in love with Laughing Eyes, Copish's daughter. The chief would not yield to Reelfoot's entreaties of marriage, however, not even after an offer of many beaver skins and the finest mussel pearls. Reelfoot was warned in a dream that he must not steal a wife but he ignored the Great Spirit. He kidnapped Laughing Eyes and carried her to the Chickasaw country. During the wedding festivities the Great Spirit stamped his foot in anger. The earth trembled. The Father of Waters rolled over Reelfoot's village. Beneath the lake that was formed rest the mortal remains of Reelfoot, his bride, and all his people. So the Chickasaw reconciled nature and human nature.

For years the Reelfoot region remained almost solely the domain of fishermen, hunters, and trappers who discovered the variety of fish and small game that flourished in this wild jumble of debris, water and land rearranged by nature. In 1908, however, a conflict to determine private or public control of Reelfoot Lake brought a social upheaval that paralleled that of the New Madrid earthquake almost a century earlier. A number of local citizens, feeling that they were being overrun by outside developers and entrepreneurs, organized bands of night riders and whipped, terrorized and finally murdered in their desperate effort to maintain a way of life they wished to keep free of outside control. Today Reelfoot Lake is a game preserve, guarded by brooding cypress and stark skeletons of trees. There is little enhancing "development" around its shores.

If Reelfoot represents Tennessee's newest natural landscape, the mountains at the opposite end of the state are mementoes of the oldest era of earth's formation. For those who can read the rocks their story unfolds in many layered cross-sections where distorted formations are exposed.

The Roan is one of these mountains. Astride the border between northeastern Tennessee and northwestern North Carolina it stands 6,286 feet tall, rising more than 4,000 feet above its immediate surroundings. Hardwoods and conifers cover its slopes. But the uniqueness of the Roan, as local people call it, is its summit—not rough and rocky but six miles of luxuriant rolling meadows. This is one of the mysterious "balds" that are fairly common in the Southern Appalachians, mountain pinnacles blanketed with a rich cover of grass and shrubs rather than the forests that top their neighboring peaks. Science and legend have offered a variety of conjectures about these open green spaces—but no single one fully explains their presence and persistence. The glory of the Roan, however, is the rhododendron that turns the meadow on its summit each June into a vast wonderland of pink and purple, rose and lavender blossoms. The Catawba rhododendron, a member of the heath family, kissing-cousin to Scotch heather, flourishes in the acid soil on these cool, cloud-drenched, windswept heights. Gnarled trunks may grow as tall as 15 feet and support clumps of limbs that bear seven or eight hundred blossoms. The accuracy of the name from the Greek—rhodon for "rose" and dendron for "tree"—becomes vividly apparent as the hundreds of acres burst into lavish bloom.

General John T. Wilder who had come to Tennessee with the Union troops during the Civil War returned after Appomatox and built a hotel he called Cloudland on the Roan. Its spacious views of distant mountain ranges and its rambling verandas attracted a variety of patrons. They ranged from botanists who were fascinated by the rich plant life of the region (Andre Michaux in 1794 provided the first record of a white person on the Roan) to lowland refugees from heat and mosquitoes. All those who came to Cloudland could boast that they slept in one state and dined in another. Visitors enjoyed the blazing log fires that rainy days and chilly evenings could make necessary even in summertime. Occasionally they wrote home about the wind that assaulted this mountain height, reporting that its ferocity made the loose boards and sturdy timbers of the hotel creak and groan like a ship at sea. The hotel no longer exists and the only corridors on the Roan today are those carpeted with grass and moss and ferns winding between the luxuriant rhododendron.

Neighbor to the Roan and the Unaka Range, along the southeastern boundary of Tennessee, the crest of the Great Smoky Mountains runs like a rugged spine some 70 miles between Tennessee and North Carolina. Along this towering ridge are 16 peaks rising more than 6,000 feet high. Plants ranging from protected coves upward to these altitudes include in the space of a few vertical miles representatives of southern and Canadian forests. Birds can migrate vertically here, seeking out the valleys in winter and returning to cool spruce-covered heights in summer.

Within the park's some 800 square miles are 200,000 acres of virgin hardwood, one of the largest stands remaining in America. There are 50,000 acres of red spruce and these include specimens more than four centuries old. It is the yellow poplar, or tulip tree, that grows to the largest size of any tree in the park. Some of the 3,500 species of plant life in the Smokies today owe their presence to the gradual pace of the glaciers that once covered much of the United States but reached only as far south as Ohio. The fingers of ice that pushed across the land some one million years ago killed all the plants in their reach—except for those that found a haven on the heights of the Southern Appalachians. Later, as the glaciers retreated,

these mountains became nature's seed-bed as some of the immigrant plants gradually returned to their northern homes.

Today the Great Smoky Mountains National Park, created in 1934, has more visitors than any other national park in our U.S. Park system. And none is more enchanted by its wonders than was one of its very first visitors, the Philadelphia botanist William Bartram, whose excitement would be echoed by travelers for generations to come. In the spring of 1775, against the advice of experienced Indian observers, he went into the country of the Overhill Cherokee where traders and soldiers had previously been the chief white visitors, and he reveled in all that he found. Part of his legacy to later generations was his description and naming of the azaleas he discovered. On first beholding hillsides a-bloom with orange and yellow clusters of flowers "suddenly opening to view from dark shades," Bartram wrote, "we are alarmed with the apprehension of the hills being set on fire." Little wonder that he recorded, "The epithet fiery I annex to this celebrated species of azalea, as being expressive of the appearance in flower."

The land of smoke, the Indians called these mountains, and when white settlers came they understood the accuracy of that description for the soft blue haze that often wraps the summits from view. They adopted the name. Unfortunately for the Cherokees the white people also wanted to adopt the land. One of Tennessee's leaders who led the movement for Indian removal was Andrew Jackson, before and during his presidency. Jackson might stand as the prototype of those Scotch-Irish settlers who dominated the opening up of the Southern Appalachians. They were really Scotch, of course, having spent only a sojourn on James 1 plantations in northern Ireland where they developed the farms and the wool industry with such success that the English hedged them about with discriminatory laws to lessen their competition. Hard-working, tenacious, proud, inventive, the Scotch-Irish were survivors. Protestant to the core, they were reputed to keep the Sabbath and anything else they could lay their hands on. In the southern highlands of America they found a wilderness that appeared to them to be largely empty and unused. Twice dispossessed—in Scotland and Ireland—of land they had tilled and improved for generations, believing in possession of land as a passionate tenet of faith, they were determined to hold this new homeland. The Cherokees, who had adopted many of the white ways, were also devoted to the land. Their genius, Sequoyah, born in the Tennessee country, had given them a written language; they could publish their own newspaper and exchange ideas in writing. And although one group yielded to the might of the federal and state governments and went west, some 15,000 refused to leave the hills and valleys, streams and woods inhabited by the spirits of their mythical creatures and the memories of their dead ancestors. During the spring and early summer of 1838 the U.S. Army began rounding up these reluctant emigrants and marched them into stockades. James Mooney, in a U.S. Ethnological Report, later summarized the scene: "The history of the Cherokee removal of 1838, as gleaned by the author from the lips of actors in the tragedy, may well exceed in grief and pathos any other passage in American history. Even the much-sung exile of the Acadians falls far behind it in its sum of death and misery . . . Families at dinner were startled by the sudden gleam of bayonets in the doorway and rose up to be driven with blows and oaths along the weary miles of trail that led to the stockade. Men were seized in the fields or going along the road, women were taken from their wheels and children from their play. In many cases, on turning for one last look as they crossed the ridge, they saw their homes in flames, fired by the lawless rabble that followed on the heels of the soldiers to loot and pillage. . . . One old patriarch, when thus surprised, calmly called his children and grandchildren around him, and, kneeling down, bid them pray with him in their own language, while the astonished soldiers looked on in silence. Then rising he led the way into exile. A woman, on finding the house surrounded, went to the door and called up the chickens to be fed for the last time, after which, taking her infant on her back and her two other children by the hand, she followed her husband with the soldiers."

The Trail of Tears it was called, the long path they followed from Tennessee and Georgia westward to Oklahoma. Some 4,000 never reached the final destination. It was a terrible toll, leaving one-fourth of a nation dead of winter's cold, hunger, disease, or escaped or killed by soldiers along the way. One small group of refugees fled to the high fastnesses of the Great Smokies and finally received from the U.S. government permission to remain there. Their descendants live there today, on the Qualla Reservation on the North Carolina side of the Great Smokies.

The pioneers had received much from the Cherokees besides their land. They shared knowledge of crops and herbs and animals and weather, medicinal cures, dyes and skills in woodworking, fashioning baskets and pots from native materials, plus using the surrounding world of nature for necessities that could also be handsome artifacts. Their bequest also included the musical names, especially of rivers: Tennessee and Hiwasee and Tellico, Tuckaleechee and Cataloochee.

With the arrival of a national park, descendants of some of these early settlers were forced to move once more. Today there remain in the park remnants of the hard, self-sufficient, satisfying life that flourished here: dog-trot cabins containing two rooms connected by a sheltered breezeway, sturdy frame houses and water-powered wheels patiently turning giant millstones, a log schoolhouse, a small white church companioned by a grassy cemetery whose worn stones bear names that sun and rain have largely erased. And around the dwellings are the clusters of barns, smokehouses, pig-pens, chicken coops, springhouses, that were part of the web of life on these lonely, landlocked little farms. These are the structures that have been preserved or restored. Many have disappeared. Driving along the highway that climbs from the tourist mecca of Gatlinburg at the Park's northwestern entrance, with its frantic blend of the authentic and the tawdry, to the summit near Clingman's Dome, or walking along many of the trails that lead to hidden waterfalls and valleys, a vistor may still be surprised to stumble upon the ruins of a stone chimney or a clump of lilac in early spring bloom and realize that a cabin once stood here.

Just as Tennessee was the first state admitted to the Union that had been carved out of a territory, so the Great Smokies became the first national park that was a gift of the states (Tennessee and North Carolina) and individuals, comprising school children who contributed dimes and quarters, generous citizens, and the Laura Spelman Rockefeller Foundation which gave $5 million to the United States; it was not a creation from the public domain.

In addition to its seasonal pageant of flowering plants; from delicate trillium in the early damp woods of spring, and dogwood splashing the hillsides with gleaming white, to the shining waxy green clumps of galax and laurel in the winter woods; there are other lives that flourish in the Great Smokies. The park is home to 50 types of animals, including the black bears whose pan-handling along the main thoroughfares frequently leads to "bear-jams," and sometimes to injuries for the foolhardy who have not heeded park warnings that the big, furry, clumsy appearing animals are really wild animals and not to be fed. There are 80 types of fish in the park, 600 miles of trout streams and 500 miles of hiking trails. There are no still waters, no lakes or ponds in the Great Smokies. Thus land and water once again provide contrast: the majesty of the mountains arising from their apparent steadfastness, while the very streams along their slopes and valleys are incessantly carving a new countenance.

The hills that were once barriers to the outside world are now attractions that bring in the outside world. At first it was the rivers that were the highways. With more than 2,100 miles of major rivers and streams lacing the state, Tennessee achieved a balanced establishment of cities among its three major geographic divisions, each city's location determined in part by its relationship to a major river.

Knoxville began as a fort located where the French Broad River, having cut through the gorges of North Carolina and wound across part of east Tennessee, joins the Holston coming out of Virginia to form the Tennessee River. One historian has said, "Of all the great rivers east of the Mississippi, it has been least friendly to civilization. Until the advent of the Tennessee Valley Authority it defied every human attempt at conquest." Knoxville is headquarters for the TVA whose giant stairway of dams and lakes not only harnessed the wild erratic river but altered the economy and destiny of an entire region. Frontiersmen who met the challenge of the Tennessee joked that they had to be half horse, half alligator, while later claims added qualities of frog, snapping turtle, raccoon, and buffalo. Knoxville flourished as Tennessee began to discover the minerals that would make it today the nation's biggest producer of marble, zinc, and ceramic clay.

By 1840 the valley farmlands surrounding Knoxville were helping make Tennessee the greatest corn producing state in the Union, securing the nickname of "hog and hominy state." Transporting that crop to the Atlantic seaboard markets posed a major challenge and brought into existence one of the colorful enterprises of the state's history, the livestock drives that flourished from around 1800 until the 1880's when railroads penetrated the mountain barriers with their swifter, more efficient means of transportation. Mules, cattle, turkeys, ducks, and especially hogs by the thousands made up these droves. It was a rowdy, colorful business. Stands, or taverns, were built along the muddy, dusty road leading to the plantations of South Carolina where cotton growers needed the food provided by the livestock growers to the west. At the height of the drives, which took place in the autumn of the year, a stand might accommodate droves of hundreds of animals accompanied by their owners, the drovers, who usually rode horseback and superintended operations, and perhaps a dozen or more hired drivers who walked the long miles and urged the animals on. To feed this river of livestock many steep hillsides that should have remained forested were cleared and planted to corn. It was the familiar story of response to an immediate necessity laying the foundation for future disaster. Some of the acres whose topsoil was destroyed by this ill-suited cropping only regained their green cover, healing the erosion of decades, with the arrival of TVA and other conservation agencies of the 1930's and 1940's.

Knoxville today represents an interesting blend of the rural and urban, conservative and progressive. Major influences are the University of Tennessee, chartered as Blount College in 1794, the TVA, and nearby Oak Ridge with its unique history and gathering of scientific expertise. There is also the impact of the millions of tourists who flow through this gateway to the Great Smokies. But along the Market Square of the downtown mall, mountain men and women still bring plants and flowers to sell—wild trillium and pink lady's slipper along with commercial nursery plants—and herbs and sometimes home canned fruits and vegetables: purple pickled beets, beans pickled in a salty brine, okra, wild blackberries.

South of Knoxville, where the Tennessee River yields to Lookout Mountain, sweeps around its base and begins a lariat-like loop across Alabama before reentering the state near Shiloh, the city of Chattanooga hugs the river and climbs surrounding mountain and ridge. Here again the ancient geological heritage reasserts itself as river is thwarted by mountain and "foams, roars and boils" on its passage through the rocky defile. Early boatmen gave this stretch of dangerous water several names, such as the Boiling Pot and the Frying Pan, but the one most common was the Suck. Thomas Jefferson used that name when he described the area: "Above the Chickamauga towns is a whirlpool called the Sucking pot, which takes in trunks of trees or boats, and throws them out again half a mile below. It is avoided by keeping very close to the bank on the south side."

When the Civil War erupted, Chattanooga had not yet made up its mind whether it would be a village or a city, but it had promoted railroad construction. River and railroad made it a strategic site during the war. The campaigns around Chattanooga were among the bloodiest fought in the south. The "battle above the clouds," on the slopes of Lookout Mountain where the soldiers wearing both the blue and the gray were "wrapped in a seamless mantle of fog," was only one of several unique engagements in the vicinity.

Following the war Chattanooga had an influx of visitors who came to look at the sites of the great battles. A number of Union soldiers who had found the countryside and the climate to their liking returned in peacetime to make their homes in the burgeoning town. An iron industry was developing, too, and this attracted business entrepreneurs. The spirit of the time and of the town received an unusual salute from an editor in Knoxville who wrote, "Chattanooga has more backbone for its size and advantages than any small village we know of. She has as many lives as a cat. As to killing her, even the floods have failed. You may knock the breath out of her—that's all. She will re-fill her lungs and draw a longer breath than ever. Her pluck has saved her and is likely to make her one of the most flourishing and prosperous cities in the South."

Textiles, chemicals, clothing, paper and leather products, fabricated metals and machinery, the rise of the chicken-and-egg business in a changing agricultural picture, and the early establishment of an industry called the Coca-Cola Bottling Company have contributed to make a present-day reality out of that editor's predictions.

When Adolph S. Ochs arrived in Chattanooga on the first day of April, 1877, the city received what may have been its single greatest asset for years to come. Certainly he became its advocate and conscience through the pages of the newspaper, The Chattanooga Times, which he acquired as a young man during the twentieth year of his life. Experience as owner and publisher of this paper, and financial perils experienced as a result of his over-enthusiastic participation in a Chattanooga cycle of boom and bust investments, led Ochs to expand from Chattanooga to New York where his New York Times became a national institution.

In the middle of Tennessee the state capital rises along the banks of the Cumberland River. Founding of the city involves an adventure that reads like fiction. In the fall and winter of 1779-80, two groups of settlers left upper East Tennessee for the distant French Lick on the Cumberland River. One group, driving horses, cattle, and sheep, traveled overland through the wilderness under the leadership of a staunch, resourceful, respected explorer-settler named James Robertson. Soon after they arrived at their destination the snows and ice ushered in a season that came to be recorded in history as the Cold Winter. Their suffering was eclipsed by that of the second party, however, journeying by water under the leadership of John Donelson, whose teen-age daughter, Rachel, would become Andrew Jackson's beloved wife. The flotilla of 30 flatboats, dugouts, and canoes carried 200 men, children, and women—several of whom were pregnant—as well as animals and household furnishings.

Led by Donelson's boat, the Adventure, they departed Fort Patrick Henry at the present site of Kingsport on December 22, 1779, floated down the Holston to the Tennessee, down and up the Tennessee to the Ohio, up the Ohio to the Cumberland, and then along that river to the French Salt-Springs and the little fort where they arrived April 24, 1780. During those months along their thousand mile journey they experienced frost and freeze and rainstorm and snow, smallpox and Indian attacks, destruction of boats and cargo, and death of several of the party. Actually no precise figure remains of the people that were declared missing but at least 33 were either drowned, frozen, killed, or captured by the Indians. Little wonder that it

has been called the Mayflower voyage of the Old Southwest.

John Donelson kept a journal of the voyage of the "good boat Adventure," and from its spare, specific entries we gather the information, if not the emotion, to give us some comprehension of this experience. Perhaps one entry can suggest the torments that afflicted Donelson's party. On Wednesday, the eighth of March, he records the "tragical misfortune of poor Stuart, his family and friends, to the number of twenty eight persons. This man had embarked with us for the western Country, but his family being deseased with the small-pox, it was agreed upon between him & the Company that he should keep at some distance in the rear, for fear of the infection spreading: and he was warned each night when the encampment should take place by the sound of a horn. After we had passed the Town, the Indians, having now collected to a considerable number, observing his helpless situation, singled off from the rest of the fleet, intercepted him & killed & took prisoners the whole crew, to the great grief of all the Company uncertain how soon they might share the same fate; their cries were distinctly heard by those boats in the rear."

Where the Tennessee turns especially treacherous, at the Suck near Chattanooga, a family named Jennings suffered catastrophe. Their boat was dashed onto a large rock. Indians along the shore fired upon the family as they worked to free the vessel. One of the young fellows and a black man were wounded and jumped into the water and disappeared. Mrs. Jennings, helping dislodge the boat, was nearly drowned when the boat suddenly loosed itself from the rock. Another member of the Jennings' party, a Mrs. Peyton, was not so fortunate. The baby she had given birth to the night before was killed "in the hurry and confusion," while she worked in the cold water to help free the boat.

By mid-March the situation of the voyagers was desperate. Provisions were exhausted. Hunger and fatigue were taking a terrible toll. Only Donelson's will did not falter. "I am determined to pursue my course, happen what will," he declared. Shortly afterward a buffalo was killed and meat filled the pots on the campfires for a little while. Herbs with which to make "sallad" were picked along the river banks, and they killed wild swan "which was very delicious." On April 24 they arrived at their destination: "a few log Cabbins which have been built on a Cedar Bluff above the Lick by Capt. Roberson and his company."

That cluster of cabins grew into the Wall Street of the South, as Nashville, with its present insurance and banking interests, sometimes calls itself. It is also, of course, Music City, sending the multi-million dollar "Nashville Sound" across America and around the world. They come from the lonesome coves and little upland farms and rocky fields and small towns, the byways and the crossroads linked by the cement ribbons of rolling Interstates, to help create that sound. If it has changed over the years, become a blend of metropolitan professionalism and rural yearning, naive romance and shrewd commercialism, perhaps its success reveals the persistence of legendary hopes and hardships that were part of the settlements on the western waters.

In the southwestern corner of Tennessee is Memphis. The Mississippi River gave this inland city an international experience from its very beginning, helped determine that it would become the largest city in the state and a distribution center for the surrounding mid-South area. Memphis now ships more hardwood than does any other U.S. port, and one-third of all the cotton grown in the United States is brokered and processed in Memphis markets.

During its earliest years Memphis was under strong Spanish influence reaching up from New Orleans. There was an interlude when leaders in the Tennessee country, unable to secure military protection, economic aid, political recognition, or even sympathy for their isolated situation, considered relying on Spanish markets and commerce via the Mississippi Valley. Such schemes were aborted and even drew charges of treason against their perpetrators, but they indicated the problems inherent in a geography that was both eastern and western in its needs and alliances. As the frontier moved from the Atlantic seaboard to the Mississippi Valley, Tennessee became a borderland between the two. It was no accident that the first president representing a western challenge to the political leadership of New England and Virginia should come from Tennessee in the person of Andrew (Old Hickory) Jackson.

Memphis had difficult beginnings. Andrew Jackson, continually embroiled in arguments, feuds, and duels, played a part in this controversy, too. His role in securing a Chickasaw Indian treaty for the land and his part in planning the layout for the town was severely criticized. And Memphis had continuing problems: the Civil War and its aftermath was devastating to the economy; three yellow fever epidemics reaped a toll in the thousands, with the last epidemic alone taking 5,000 lives; there was financial failure; when Ole Man River went on the rampage there was the devastation of flood. But the rich bottomlands that the river had nourished with silt over the centuries continued to produce their abundant crops; trade recovered and prospered; jazz came up-river from New Orleans; cypress and oak and other hardwoods went down-river from the inland forests; cotton began to move west as soybeans and pastures diversified the crops; Memphis was a crossroads for it all. And Beale Street, in the heart of the city, became a special kind of crossroads. It was here in the early 1900's that a black man named W. C. Handy wrote and played some of those distinctive songs that became known as "the blues." His *Beale Street Blues* sang of the "tailor-mades and hand-me-downs" that mingled along these sidewalks and in these stores and taverns; the "hognose restaurants and chitterling cafes;" the "jugs that tell of by-gone days" and the river that still ran wet even when "Beale's done gone dry." On Beale Street, too, successful black lawyers, realtors, politicians, and at least one nationally known writer, George Lee, mingled with "conjure" doctors, pawnbrokers, and gamblers. Wide-eyed visitors from the surrounding rural countryside of western Tennessee and nearby Mississippi thronged Beale Street on Saturday afternoons and evenings. Pewee's Place was a gathering spot for musicians. From the De Soto Fish Dock on the Mississippi River to East Street, old Beale Street was one mile of commerce, folklore, entertainment, chicanery, food, drink, and music unlike any other in the country. Unfortunately, Memphis allowed this landmark to fall into decay and virtually disappear. Yet in its heyday it helped produce one of America's few indigenous musical sounds. Moan a new blues for the demise of Old Beale Street's memory, Mr. Handy!

Rivers were created by nature but those other arteries of commerce and communication, the roads, were man's handiwork. They determined the development of agriculture and industry, the location of towns and cities, and the outcome of struggles with nature and human nature. In Tennessee, with its varied and often forbidding geography, the building of roads became and remains one of the crucial challenges of progress, balancing obvious immediate needs and benefits with long-term, sometimes hidden costs.

Two of Tennessee's most picturesque and important highways of history are commemorated today in our national park system: the Wilderness Road at Cumberland Gap and the Natchez Trace Parkway south of Nashville.

Buffalo were the early engineers of America and their plodding hoofs trampled out the paths that the tread of Indian moccasins beat down farther in journeys of trade and warfare across the land. As explorers and Long Hunters ventured into the wild interior of the country they followed these trails wherever possible. One of the earliest of these thoroughfares came to be known as the Wilderness Trail. This loosely connected system of pioneer paths reached from the Potomac River to the Falls of the Ohio. At Cumberland Gap the trail swung down from Virginia, looped across part of Tennessee and led into the "dark and bloody ground" of Kentucky.

Cumberland Gap (it probably would have been called a "notch" in New England or a "pass" in the West) provided a gateway through the formidable Appalachian chain of mountains thrust up like a massive wall against westward expansion. It remains an impressive landmark today, inviting the traveler to pause and stand near the summit and look out upon the green forests and blue mountain ranges of three adjoining states. On these heights and through this passage historic dramas have unfolded. Along the narrow, hazardous Wilderness Road, initially blazed by Daniel Boone and 30 hardy axmen, and through this gap poured some 300,000 pioneers during one brief interval from 1775 to 1800.

On the fog-shrouded heights of the gap and up and down the winding miles of the road, soldiers in Union blue and Confederate grey fought from 1861 till 1864 for control of what seemed a strategic site in the western theater of the Civil War. During the last decade of the nineteenth century English capitalists promoted a feverish period of mineral and land speculation in the Cumberland Gap area of the Wilderness Road. Failure of this boom probably marked the transition from a pioneer period whose customs and habits still remained alive in surrounding hills and coves, to a modern day when motor cars sweep effortlessly along the route of the old Wilderness Road and across the saddle of Cumberland Gap where a Holiday Inn now accommodates restless travelers.

The authoritative historian of the American frontier, Frederick Jackson Turner, summarized the successive waves of migration that passed this way and left their mark on America's history: "Stand at Cumberland Gap," he wrote, "and watch the procession of civilization, marching single file—the buffalo following the trail to the salt springs, the Indian, the fur-trader and hunter, the cattle-raiser, the pioneer farmer—and the frontier has passed by."

Another road winding through history and legend was the Natchez Trace, halfway across Tennessee from the Wilderness Road. The Trace—old French for "a line of footprints"—stretched 500 miles from Nashville, Tennessee to Natchez, Mississippi. Today the parkway that follows its course preserves both human and natural history. Along the pleasantly graded, well-tended highway underbrush has been cleared, historical sites have been marked and in some instances restored; the roadsides are manicured. But at parking places where paths lead into woods or meadows it is possible to leave the asphalt thoroughfare and turn aside to a sunken corridor, sometimes carpeted in rotting leaf-mulch under tall old trees, which marks the worn route of the Trace itself.

The Trace was born of the river. Those first Americans who pushed across the Appalachians into Tennessee and on to Kentucky and Indiana, as well as those in the western reaches of Pennsylvania, sent their products—flour, tobacco, hides and furs, millstones, iron, hemp and Monongahela whiskey—down the rivers along which they settled to join the Mississippi and find a ready market at one of its ports. Natchez, with its mansions on the bluffs and its gambling, frolicking Natchez-Under-the-Hill along the river, became one of the busiest, liveliest landings above New Orleans. The frontiersmen tied up their rafts and keelboats and barges and sold their back-country goods and, if they were of stern character or in good luck, headed home with cash in their pockets. They could not fight the Mississippi back up-river, however, and so they sold their vessels for timber and headed for home. On horseback or on foot, by way of the Trace and Nashville they traveled from their markets to their farms.

The "Kaintucks" these keelboat men and rafters were called, no matter what their native state might be, and as they trudged homeward they were often victims of thieves and highwaymen. From about 1785 through much of the next century the Natchez Trace provided a colorful panorama of American history. The Kaintucks were joined by throngs of others: adventurers and settlers, murderers and missionaries, slaves and soldiers, gamblers and politicians. The hunters and the hunted, the rascals and the heroes all helped win the Trace its popular nickname: the Devil's Backbone.

The most popular figure associated with the Trace was Andrew Jackson. In 1791 he brought his beloved Rachel along its miles after one of the most controversial marriages in American history. Years later, during the War of 1812, a haggard and angry Jackson marched with his dispirited troops along the Trace and won the nickname that stayed with him all his life, Old Hickory. After the Battle of New Orleans in January, 1815, Jackson rode the Trace as a victor, gloriously greeted at Nashville and at his home, the Hermitage. It was a triumphant march that would end at the White House in 1828—but without Rachel, who lay buried in the garden of Hermitage.

At one park along the Tennessee route of the Trace today there stands a simple stone shaft, rough and unfinished at its summit. It represents a life cut off in its prime. No episode of the Trace's history remains more shrouded in mystery than the death of Meriwether Lewis, heroic partner of the famous Lewis and Clark expedition. In October, 1809, Lewis was serving as Governor of upper Louisiana, having been appointed to the post during Thomas Jefferson's presidency. On his way from St. Louis to Washington, Lewis stopped at Grinder's Stand, southwest of Nashville, to spend the night. This was a gloomy, heavily wooded stretch of the Trace and when Meriwether Lewis died of gunshot wounds suffered during the hours after midnight rumors mushroomed. Had Lewis' acknowledged melancholia driven him to suicide, as Mrs. Grinder said in her account of finding the wounded man? Or was Grinder's Stand a haven of murderers and robbers as were some of the other taverns along this lonely, foreboding route? The answer is buried along the Natchez Trace.

History might happen along our highways and trails but memory and tenor of the events and people, the spirit of place set in a context of time, has often been transmitted in humble places: at winter firesides, haven against slashing rain or sudden snow; on summer verandahs shaded by wisteria vines or hidden behind aged boxwood bushes; on courthouse lawns; around hunters' campfires; at sick beds during lonely vigils.

The climate, the landscape, the history of the people who settled and remained in Tennessee all combined to create a story-telling, singing people—whether their songs were the ballads of the mountains or the blues of the lowlands or today's country music. As for the stories, one asset Tennessee has enjoyed in full measure is a generous helping of tall tales and folk heroes and heroines. Many of these were real people. Others are offspring of a union of fact and fancy, men and women made larger than life to capture the attention of listeners and win laughter or tears, wonder or fear.

One of the state's good listeners, James R. Aswell, evoked the atmosphere in which yarns were once spun and memories were refurbished and imparted to others. "Every small county seat town in Tennessee," he said, "has its Liars' Bench, gathering place for the local historians, yarn-spinners, and wags. In the heat and good fellowship of the long summer afternoons, talk for the pure sake of talking blossoms at its most extravagant. At the Liars' Bench you will find lawyers and merchants, Negroes and whites, topers and preachers, and they all know how to tell a story. They have on tongue's-tip a great source of oral literature...

"Though most Liars' Bench tales probably sprout from some kernel of fact, each teller garnishes them with fancies of his own, interpolates bits of personal experience, and borrows heavily from accounts of other events and personages about which he has a fuller stock of hearsay. Thus, a tale which originates in East Tennessee may cross the state and, after countless tellings, reach West Tennessee dressed in a wholly different set of circumstances and with only the plot-germ intact."

The freedom allowed to the tale-teller left the imagination unfettered to wander through many unexpected and revealing labyrinths. Heroes and heroines created at the Liars' Bench suggested the virtues and values that were held in greatest public esteem, for there was little hypocrisy at this gathering place. It was a male stronghold. Women found their events and places to share stories and spin yarns closer to home and in gatherings at church and little community school, institutions they helped establish and kept in thriving condition.

Who were some of the boisterous and the meek, the mettlesome and the craven who were kept alive by the storytellers? The terrible Harpes, Big and Little, who ranged across Tennessee and along the Natchez Trace, with 38 murders to their score before Big Harpe was captured, hung, and his head was impaled on a post along the highway as a warning to other evil-doers. There was the Bell Witch, so called because she tormented members of the Bell family in Robertson County during the early years of the 19th century. Her real identity was supposed to be Kate Batts, no thin old crone but a plump, often pleasant, woman who lived in the neighborhood. In her disguise as an invisible spirit, however, she set rooms topsy-turvy, shifted furniture, spilled food, and made life generally miserable for her victims. Even Andrew Jackson failed in his effort to solve the riddle of the Bell Witch and after a night spent at the house she haunted he abdicated in her favor.

The industry or craft or art of manufacturing moonshine whiskey has given rise to some favorite tall tale characters, among them Mahala Mullins. She was a Melungeon, one of the isolated and interesting colony of people who live in a particularly inaccessible area of upper East Tennessee. Their unknown national and racial identity gave rise to many theories concerning their origin: descendants of shipwrecked Portuguese who found their way into the Appalachians centuries ago? Remnants of Sir Walter Raleigh's Lost Colony from Roanoke Island along the Atlantic Coast? People of mixed African and Indian and European descent? Their outcast status pushed them to the poorest upland farms, forcing some of the community to distill their corn into illegal but profitable whiskey. One of the moonshiners never arrested by the federal revenue officers was Mahala Mullins, although she dispensed her product openly and plentifully from her own rocking chair. She won immunity from the law because of her weight. Some said she tilted the scales at 400 pounds but other estimates went as high as 700 pounds. In any case, she was too heavy to be transported off the mountain where her cabin was perched and when an energetic officer devised a way to have her hauled down the hillside and to the county jail it was discovered that she was altogether too massive to pass through the front entrance to her house. The law prohibited any damage to the dwelling in the course of her arrest. "Here I am. Take me if you can," Mahala said, and kept on selling her Mason jars of white lightning. And when she died, the fireplace had to be knocked out of the end of her kitchen so her body could be removed for burial.

Other people and events had firmer foundation in fact than the Bell Witch and Mahala Mullins. There was the engineer, Casey Jones, who could make a locomotive whistle cry and moan, who opened the throttle and refused to jump when he died in his train's wreck and was buried at the town of Jackson. Dozens of versions of Casey Jones' ballad became part of Southern folklore. There was Ed Crump of Memphis, "Boss" to the people of his city and state for his role in politics, who was the subject of at least one blues song and dozens of stories. He fulfilled the image his title as "Boss Crump" created. For instance, in one hotly contested political race he said of his opponent: "In the art galleries of Paris there are 27 pictures of Judas Iscariot—none look alike but all resemble Gordon Browning." Such a man, Crump thundered, "would milk his neighbor's cow through a crack in the fence." And there was the mystery of Sam Houston, frontiersman, teacher, Greek scholar who could recite pages of The Iliad as he rode through the Tennessee wilds, adopted by the Cherokees who gave him the name, The Raven. Why did he suddenly resign his office after he was elected Governor of Tennessee and head West, for Texas? The question has never been answered.

And there was Mother Jones, good for dozens of stories, who lost her husband and her four children in the yellow fever epidemic in Memphis in 1867 and spent the rest of her hundred years, until her death in 1930, fighting against child labor and for prison reform, organizing labor unions, especially in the Appalachian coal fields. Plump, pert, bespectacled, often wearing dressy black even when she was in jail, Mother Jones was a fiery orator. "Fight like hell till you go to heaven," she charged. And when asked about her home she said, "I reside where there is a good fight against wrong."

Tennessee is called the "Volunteer State," a name won because of its response to wrongs, real or imagined. East Tennessee mountaineers who had drafted one of the nation's first manifestos of independence volunteered for the battle of Kings Mountain and helped win a decisive victory that culminated at Yorktown in the Revolutionary War. When President James K. Polk called for 50,000 men from all the nation in the Mexican War of 1846, Tennessee alone sent more than 30,000 volunteers (the state quota was 2,800). An American folk hero of World War I was mild-mannered Alvin C. York who had learned his marksmanship hunting squirrels in Tennesse woods. On October 8, 1918, armed with a pistol and a rifle, this farmer who had once registered as a conscientious objector to war, killed 25 Germans, captured 132 more and put 35 machine guns out of action.

Despite their readiness to volunteer for a fight, an innate sense of personal dignity, even courtesy, has also been part of Tennessee character. The famous World War II correspondent Ernie Pyle observed this when he was stationed in England with some Tennessee boys. This self-taught judge of men said, "It seems to me that these boys feel more at home over here than any of the other troops . . . I defy you to find more real gentlemen among our troops than in a camp of these so-called hillbillies. There is a simple genuineness about them that shows in every word they speak. They are courteous, friendly, and trusting—all by instinct."

Instinct has often been the guide for Tennesseans' response to major challenges. In the more complex and interdependent world of today and tomorrow, where every choice and relationship affects a whole web of succeeding choices and associated relationships, there is need for more thoughtful and informed response. Self-discipline in the wise use of natural resources and in human rivalries and adjustments are as vital to Tennessee as to all the nation. Changes demanding such discipline have accrued slowly and surely through the years.

A visitor to Tennessee once asked, "How far is it from Oak Ridge to the Great Smoky Mountains?"

The answer came back, "About a hundred years."

Thus this place and its people are poised between yesterday and tomorrow. In the shadow of mountains that are among the ancients of the earth, physicists and laborers at the Manhattan Project helped usher in the Atomic Age. Giant industries, dams, highways, and strip developments expand across a landscape where it is still possible to find clear, rushing streams, still meadows, deep woods. But the very abundance of nature seems often to have encouraged a carelessness among those who enjoy her bounty. Pollution of the rivers along which so much history has unfolded, blighting of the earth through massive gougings for its treasures and individual littering of its open spaces and hidden havens, wasteful and trivial use of its mineral and forest and land resources: these are immediate and imperative challenges. If Tennessee responds to this summons as readily as to past musters, creatively seeking new relationships with nature and with other people, it will bring fresh luster to its title of the Volunteer State.

Choices confronting Tennesseans accumulate relentlessly, insistently. They involve the survival or ruin of a varied, ancient, and irreplaceable landscape spread like a feast from the mountains to the Mississippi. Words remembered from a highland ballad might serve as a useful touchstone in future deliberations: "O, green grows the laurel, and so does the rue . . ."